The Favorite

Critical Reviews

Lucinda Watson's poems are upsetting in the way that powerful poetry always is: The images are sensuous and provocative, but also suggestive of pain and regret. A charmed, privileged life—deconstructed.

David Ignatius, columnist for the *Washington Post* and author of *The Paladin*.

***

Poetry as memoir and memoir as poetry—Lucinda Watson brings both together to take us with her on a truly captivating life journey.

Peter Andreas, Brown University, author of *Killer High: A History of War in Six Drugs*

***

The Favorite is an arrow to the heart.

Cig Harvey, internationally acclaimed photographer, author of *You An Orchestra You A Bomb*

***

Lucinda Watson's engrossing collection, *The Favorite*, is a sweeping exploration of what it is to be a daughter, a lover, and a woman. Watson's potent, and often-witty insights, are spun through with unexpected imagery. One important thread is her private rebellion and deepening self-awareness as she explores her relationship with her powerful father. These are skillfully wrought, deeply insightful poems of humanity, sexuality and loss.

Brett Hall Jones, Director of the Community of Writers at Squaw Valley

***

Lucinda Watson's *The Favorite* is a remarkable debut collection. These finely crafted poems begin with a passionate and, at times, uncomfortable exploration of family relationships. There is privilege, travel; and the frequent trips she takes as a child continue literally and metaphorically into adulthood, motherhood and difficult relationships. Every poem seems effortless with graceful lines, affectionate tones, and lucid eloquence. The illumination at the center of even the darkest poems transcend loss in all its forms and celebrates the wonder and reward of simply being human.

Kevin Pilkington, Sarah Lawrence College, author of *The Unemployed Man Who Became a Tree*

The Favorite

by

Lucinda Watson

Golden Antelope Press
715 E. McPherson
Kirksville, Missouri 63501
2020

ISBN: 978-1-936135-98-1

Library of Congress Control Number: 2020941573

Published by:
Golden Antelope Press
715 E. McPherson
Kirksville, Missouri 63501

Available at:
Golden Antelope Press
715 E. McPherson
Kirksville, Missouri, 63501
Phone: (660) 665-0273
http://www.goldenantelope.com
Email: ndelmoni@gmail.com

Contents

Acknowledgments   iv

Part One   1
  Road Trip   4
  Early Childhood Memory Number 7   5
  Who Put the Tiffany Paper in the Rat's Cage   6
  Our Year on a Boat   7
  A Commanding Figure   8
  Across the Pond   9
  Forbidden Rice 10
  Hiding Faith 11
  Our Front Hall 12
  The Lion Still Roars 13
  Great Aunt Helen 14
  Ritual 15
  Cocktail Hour 16
  Another Hurricane Coming 17
  Musical Chairs 18

Part Two   19
  Photograph of My Mother, circa 1935, Found in a Wall of the Cloisters
      Hotel in Sea Island, Georgia 21
  In Rome With My Dad on Business 22
  The Dress That Went to The White House 23
  The Favorite 25
  For Sale: Wedding Gown, Never Worn 26
  Riding in Ireland with My Dad 27
  Life 28
  Riding 29
  Remembring Isadora Duncan 30

Pay No Attention to the Man Behind the Curtain 31
Barnstorming 33
Melania 34
Letter Yet Unsent 35
Sweet Strings 36
When I Think of My Mother I See a Closed Door 37

Part Three   **39**
I've Found Her Lost Again 41
Filial Visit 42
The Wedding Veil 43
Gratitude 44
Pale 45
Sable NIght 46
Vermont: Fall's End 47
Murmuration 48
In the Desert You Can't Remember Your Pain 49
Theft 50
Conclusions are Lethal 51
Naptime 52
If I Hadn't Asked 53
1963, Connecticut, President Kennedy, Cuba and My Dad 55
North Haven Island 57
Grief 58
Love at the Car Wash 59
The Dinner 60
Interviewing 61
Creation 62
Seeing Lake Tahoe 63
I Love My Gun: A Confessional 64
Bird's Eye View of Flight 65
Thanksgiving 66
The Neighbor 67
Getting Around Town 68
Slice of Life 69
Diagnosis 70
The Great Blue Heron 71
Almost 70 72
What I Really Wanted for Breakfast 73
Under It All 74
Adoption 75

Acknowledgments:

- *The Adirondack Review*
- *The Broken Plate*
- *Cape Rock Poetry*
- *Circle Press*
- *Eunoia Review*
- *Evening Street Review*
- *The Griffin*
- *The Healing Muse*
- *Inkwell*
- *Lindenwood Review*
- *Louisville Review*
- *The MacGuffin Literary Journal*
- *Magazine, Spring*
- *Phantasmagoria*
- *Penman Review*
- *Pennsylvania English*
- *Poet Lore*
- *Prelude*
- *The Round*
- *SLAB*
- *Stickman Review*
- *Third Wednesday*
- *Umbrella Factory Magazine*
- The author is especially grateful to the Community of Writers at Squaw Valley and to Maine Media Workshops.

Part One

Charles Levis—New York

Road Trip

We are all naked in the backseat
of a 1957 Plymouth station wagon
in late June in Connecticut.
The sticky, shiny plastic has cracks that bite us.
My mother says, *It's 87 and counting.*
No one is saying a word.

White dresses are layered like doll clothes
across the wayback, and I can hear them
crackle against each other as we do at home. We
are all too hot, but Mom says, *Sit still,*
as she drives, her flamingo skirt fanned around her,
the wagon slithering
like a snake up the Merritt Parkway.

We are visiting Grandfather, and since we're never
clean enough, we'll be hauled out at a rest stop
to be straightjacketed into dresses and our mother's
hope for acceptance after nine years, six children — five
daughters, and one son, who rides
shotgun and wears what he wants.

Early Childhood Memory Number 7

My cotton dress sticks to my back and belly and
I have been hiding a long, long time.

I am trying very hard not to move or even breathe as if I do
the family of large, shiny, black ants get distracted from their

task of moving an object ten inches from its original home to a new one.
I want to be moved like that: silently and smoothly.

My skin itches but I am disciplined.
There are few noises: soft bird cries and the rustle of

leaves in the apple tree nearby.
I can hear my mother in the kitchen washing dishes.

Whoosh on, whoosh off.
I wish she would make chocolate pudding.

The ants walk back and forth, majestic in their march.
It is warm and yet cool under the leaves.

I am invisible. Invincible.
I can smell the deep, earthy smell of summer,

so rich I feel faint.

Who Put the Tiffany Paper in the Rat's Cage

A crime has been discovered on this Saturday morning.
My mother's perfectly blue like a Maine sky stationery from Tiffany's
has been used to line the rat's cage.
It's pretty clear who did this but we are lined up anyway.
In the front hall underneath the curving gallows of stairs we six stand,
not unlike the condemned in a holding pen.
We know we are all condemned no matter how this plays out.
My father stands in front of our lineup:
"One of you has committed a crime and is lying about it.
Until that person steps forward no one will leave this house."
We all know who has done this but my mother is standing behind
my father making hand signals of don't tell no matter what.
I feel like falsely confessing just so I can go to Betsey Beecher's house.
Her father is never home and her mother thinks I am interesting.

Our Year on a Boat

Our father had a gun he used to shoot
the kerosene stove in the cabin

at dinnertime on the boat.
We watched, sealed to the sticky,

red plastic banquette,
all five of us, as he clicked it

against the burner.
Click, click,

BOOM!

A relief to us if the stove ignited
rather than him.

Dinner was Dinty Moore Stew and "No
bread, girls!" and my mom did the

laundry, head hung, sudsing quietly under
the floorboards, and hung it out to

dry on wire fences around the boat.
Even our Spanky pants laid out

in plain sight in front of the whole ocean,
mine with small pink roses.

That summer we sailed through the angry Baltic,
straight on through nights locked in our bunks,

swaddled in stiff oilskins, imprisoned by childhood,
smell of kerosene ether to desperate sleep.

When we hit land each time, off we'd go,
cash clutched in chubby fingers,

Swedish word for bread in our head.
Me and my older sisters,

free at last.

A Commanding Figure

I am a commanding figure
though I am not tall. In
fact, my wrist is easily encompassed
by the talons of a hawk. He follows
me incessantly today dipping
around my person like a mad painter
with a large brush dripping, still baton-like,
in the air around us. It is my air, not his.
(I wonder when a mother hawk knows
to shove her chick from the nest?)
I am stalking the cool air,
under the hawk's wings,
walking backwards, toes down,
through the cool grass slowly.
I'm an Indian.
I may be twelve today.

Across the Pond

I used to take the old, red canoe after school before
my brother got to it, and find freedom on the pond
though it was covered in algae and fingers of weeds
that grabbed you from under.
Out I would go, a silent paddler, learned at midnight
when humans slept. Dipping into the dark water with a perfect
arc of stroke, a sliver of silver, a flash of speed,
Pocahontas with no braids, paddling to the island floating on
the lake with birch trees like antennas poking up to the sky.
 I was invisible.
The canoe always found its shelf under trees who bent down to
cover me, and my hand took the frayed, gray rope
held before by prior escapees, and wrapped a Bowline
around the harsh white and black of the bark on the tree trunk.
 I was safe.
Utterly still on the verdant moss, velvet skin to caress, lying back
softly, my hair was green, my hands were green, the camouflage
was working. It always worked.
No one could find me here.
The birches were wrapped in paper bark with messages
underneath like ancient Greek tablets only I could translate.
Sometimes it took all afternoon.
I was a stubborn child and waiting was my middle name.
Small and large ants crisscrossed my bony ankles like feathers
against skin.
A snake came and went.
There was a bird call.
 The island was so still, nothing could move it off its anchor.

I learned everything I know from that bark.

Forbidden Rice

I love forbidden
rice if you have to
ask why you are not my
friend.

Altitude isn't good for
my brain as being deprived
of anything, particularly air,
exacerbates my oppositional
defiant disorder.

I hate flagman and I don't let
them boss me around which sometimes gets me into trouble.

If there is a line
I won't get in it.

Hiding Faith

Cynthia Paterno said if I became a Catholic, I would have a cleaner
soul, so I turned my closet into an altar using books, shoe boxes,
candle stubs from the dining room, lace cloths from the top shelf
of the linen closet where I often hid, and
odd detritus found in the sewing box.
Like a squirrel hiding nuts, I hid faith.

Every night I put my hands together like Audrey Hepburn
in *The Nuns Story* and prayed.
"Please God let Betty Webster let me into her secret
club!" "Please God! Let my sister get ugly!"
"Please God! Let the dog be able to sleep in my room tonight!"
Sometimes I would put a white towel over my head and
convince myself I had Christ as a husband though I was only nine.

I never ate in there or spoke, and though I was convinced I might
hear voices I never heard a word.
I had to close the closet door carefully knowing it might
latch forever and I knew no one would look for me even at
dinnertime.

Months later or maybe
it was only a few days, my confessional
disappeared,
shoe boxes gone, candles
missing, our mother making sure
we had no faith as she never did,
and me thinking I wasn't good enough
for God.

Our Front Hall

Our front hall had a very tall grandfather clock at the foot of the stairs keeping watch over the household. No one could wind it but my father and the clock defined the nights in regular chimes reaching everyone's ears in everyone's bedroom.There was a front hall table made of lustrous mahogany where mail and packages were placed daily.The legs of the table looked like a young girl with four legs curtseying all at once. I know because I spent a lot of time under there waiting for God knows what. My favorite part however in this wonderful area of our house was the front hall closet which no one could put anything in except for my father. It was his personal closet for his overcoat and his hats and his umbrellas and his galoshes. I don't remember hearing we weren't supposed to go in the closet so I went in the closet quite a bit. There was a shelf the hats were on that had a thumbtacked piece of decorative ribbon that was ruched: something I had never seen before. I took some delight in pulling a piece of it off and seeing what it felt like. My father had four or five coats in there and most of the coats were some range of the color gray. There were cashmere coats, and wool coats, and cotton coats, and canvas coats. The coats had a big life and seemed to go out a lot. Sometimes alone, and sometimes in pairs the coats went out in the world: across oceans and in airplanes, office buildings, and houses not ours, down inside boats, outside on sidewalks. They always came back home slightly different than when they had left. I knew this because when I went in the closet I would stand up inside each coat starting with my head going into the bottom because they were buttoned up, you see, and I would shimmy myself up to usually just the lowest button because my father was very tall and I was still short. I would stand there and breathe in the outside world imagining where he had been and who he had seen and the smell of old Spice would anesthetize me against the real world. In the closet I created whatever I wanted sometimes for hours. No one ever looked for me. I stood so still inside a coat I became a part of its life.

The Lion Still Roars

When my father died
everyone ran for his stuff:
clothes and cameras–
cufflinks and chainsaws–
I got the lion,
his childhood toy.
Head dangling from a hole in the neck,
fur worn down to a gray nub.
The lion jumps when you pull its string,
it sits back ever so slowly on its haunches and
springs at you when you thought it wouldn't.

The lion learned this from a master jumper.
A slapper, a dancer, a breaker, a chewer, a crier, a liar.
Right by the bedside the lion watched and learned.

One can't repair this brain chemistry in animal or man.
Violence is just violence, after all.

My mother thinks I should have the lion repaired.
She is used to the simple act of pulling a string,
comforted by things as they were.
But the lion and I have an understanding
about the unpredictable nature of life.

Great Aunt Helen

banished to
Tryon, North Carolina,
always a spinster, never a
lover except for the time
she was caught kissing the hand
of sweet Elsie, the daughter
of the comely, black haired, upstairs
maid who was supposed to be
watching them. Banished to Tryon,
no address passed on, Great Aunt

Helen only appeared in
severe illness or stormy
weather. She made soup.

Delivered by palest, plump
hands with a painter's slop of
freckles, a *ding-dong* of indigestion.
She once told my grandmother
to break my spirit just as
hers had been. By then it was
too late.

Ritual

When my grandmother died, they laid her out
in the dusty, hazy, winter lit bedroom of her house.
The air moved in clouds around the family
milling around noiselessly.
So we could bend and kiss her goodbye,
they lined us up in one long row,
determined by sex, age and family hierarchy.
Serpentine sprawl through
long corridors lit by small monkeys
with torches for arms and watchful eyes.
I felt small,
smaller than my skin too loose over my knees, my patent leather shoes like
boats with water in them, sloshing my feet down the hall
snaking through these old rooms, a lavender tail
swishing through murky mustiness, a chamber lit by God's spotlight,
the bed, a throne.
I moved out of my body and floated above the bed
wanting to spit on her face.
Looking down I saw the gleam of her scalp through
her fine silver hair and one small, daring, ant weaving its own path.
I took out her hairpins and shook her head,
tossing it for her,
cut the laces on her shoes and threw them
one by one
out the window
and she rose and danced with me.
Danced like a wood nymph.
Waved and bounced her dress, a curtain that opened to me.
I saw her sorrow and her joy.
I saw her prison.
I kissed her hand like a butterfly would
and sent her on her journey.

Cocktail Hour

The Venetian blind is throwing itself at the window
open on this windy night.
I am waiting for it to be dinner.
Everyone is waiting in their room for my father to come home.
It is winter.
Outside my room, I have been watching two gray squirrels
in a nut race.
The bigger of the two wins.
I hear the front door close.
My mother calls out,
Your father's home.
We open our doors
to go downstairs.

Maybe nothing is going to happen tonight.

The music goes on and it is Rachmaninoff's "Concerto Number 4."

I am number four.

Upstairs in the hall there is a map of the world
in bas-relief.
I always run my fingers over it imagining I am blind.
Russia isn't as flat as one might think.
China seems to go on forever.
I wonder if all the people in China are lost all the time
and if they eat off plates.
I would like to live in China.

Another Hurricane Coming

Hurricane, hurricane:
sounds like a Negro spiritual or command to walk faster
or maybe a warning to not eat sugar
or a sigh for the world.
Hurricane creeping up the coast while we scurry
to get ready again, all while hoarding and grabbing.
The Red Cross is changing color
and the crossing guards have quit.
No one is in charge
and everyone is yelling orders.
I am looking under my bed for currency
and sitting in the audience like Schopenhauer
said, a child waiting for the curtain to rise on life.
When we were young my mother used to love storms
and would drive us out to the beach to watch them.
Get out of the car, she would say, *feel the wind, watch the waves,*
they might snatch you up. Away you would go.

Musical Chairs

I feel like we're playing musical chairs in the world.
I am not good at that game.

When I was a kid people used to scream
at me because I would never leave my chair.

If I did it was to slither

over to the next chair
before the music even thought about stopping.

In my house there are many chairs.
There are many photos.
I like to stop

and sit on the chair that looks directly into the photo
of my family surrounding me.

That's all I see
That's all I pray for.

Part Two

Photograph of My Mother, circa 1935, Found in a Wall of the Cloisters Hotel in Sea Island, Georgia

She's lying there, faintly amused, staring
at the camera from her
spot on a beach in front of an old hotel with fat
white columns too short to mean anything.
She's wearing a bathing suit slightly too large,
passed down from her cousin, Edwina,
who lives with her Grandmother Field in a
house with a cook.
She hopes she's the prettiest
girl around and knows what she's supposed to do.
"It's just as easy to fall in love with a rich man as a poor
one!" said her mother.
She has learned to sidle at the men like a spider with the most elaborate
web, all sparkly and wet,
glistening in its circle around her.
Her hair tangled into a moist cap, untamed and
dark, her worst feature her mother would say.
She practices what she's been taught, shifts her eyes,
which sometimes glisten like fish in a cold mountain stream.
She is a hungry chameleon.

She is tempting.
She will always feel alone.
She is this family's last resort,
so she can never eat dinner.

In Rome With My Dad on Business

I'm in Rome with my Dad on business,
addendum to a big, male package.
Small brown suitcase, thin high voice,
one crinkled flowered dress,
and we go out to lunch and eat
black squid and bread but no butter.
In front of us is Charles Aznavour, a movie star,
and a babe my Dad likes a lot as he
stares at her like he stares at prey.
I am almost twelve.
The lady is blond with a tight U of a skirt,
hair pushed up high into a beehive tangle.
She is silent and sits still on the back of
a Vespa, pillioned by
hierarchy and kitten heels.
I'm watching the hunt, watching and learning.
Charles Aznavour and my father are competing
but Charles doesn't know this, as he already
paid for her, but my Dad keeps his eyes on the
prize and slips wads of Roman cash in and out of his pocket
money clip flashing in the hot sun.
We go to our hotel, my Dad makes a hair appointment for me.

The Dress That Went to The White House

There's a dress in the attic that went
to the White House with my mother in it.
I go up to the attic all the time and sit on the floor inside the
dress and dance with her.
The odor of musk, cedar and silverfish are there as well as the scent
of hope.
I see her with lovely shoulders bared, the color of September even
in December,
and I hear her voice, sultry, filled with high octaves
ending on an even higher note.
I'm there with her when President Kennedy asks her to dance and I feel her
feet tap tap tapping and we slide and glide across the lacquered black floor.
It's dark when we come home and she lays her dress out on
the chaise lounge, which opens its arms
and the next day it's gone
and I find it in the attic, still fragrant, hopeful
and alive.

24

The Favorite

I was the favorite;
the pretty one.
The one chosen to travel
on long trips and
to sleep in his room,
while everyone else stayed home.

Once, my mother dressed me up
like the woman he was sleeping with.

I am still not sure what the prize was,
my sisters thought I had won.

This man my mother found for me
said to me
just last week
that older men were better off than older women
as they could be with much younger women,
while the same was not true for women.
"Women just don't measure up over time," he said.

In certain cultures, mirrors are shrouded
and women never see the light of day.
Men rape women on court orders
and have friends come along.

Each morning I examine the freshness of my face,
the fading of my footprints,
the smooth other side of the bed.

For Sale: Wedding Gown, Never Worn

They say bitterness eats at you like vinegar on wood:
until one day the floor is rough and

splintered under your feet.
They forget how touch soothes as

well as arouses, small hairs rise on an arm as the sense
of another's hand draws near.

The belly, yearning for the trail of
warm fingers, searching.

The breast, for two fingers, a twirl.
After the wedding she was invisible,

though he spoke to her, it was
in tongues.

She understood the content but not the wounds.
She believed she could seduce him

again like Molly Bloom: yes, yes, perfume all over the
bed he never slept in.

She wakes at night still calling,
"Why?"

Riding in Ireland with My Dad

I'm seven, dress already wrinkled,
standing with my hand in my dad's at the top
of the airplane stairs on the way to Ireland,
my hair band too tight—a crown of roses.
My head is cocked to one side, and I'm shyly smiling
for the story. I know my job. I'm a child sacrificed
for paternal entertainment. It's a long flight over Gander
not a goose, I hear— and Dad gives me a pill for my headache.
We land, and he rents a car, tells me to keep him awake
on our drive to Galway — where leprechauns await me.
Perched on the edge of the thin, nylon-covered seat,
my feet on the vibrating, steel-plated floor, I feel Ireland
but not safe. We sleep in a castle with harsh sheets
and the next day, Ian takes us riding.
My horse, Conroy, is 17 Hands, depending on whose—
not mine because I tried—and a leaper.

My dad bought me a new riding jacket gnarled
with tweed, and I'm wearing an Irish riding hat sloshy
on my small head. We walk our horses down
a brown, rutted path, mine stepping in and over rock
and roots and swaying like a hammock.
Dad says to Ian, "Can you jump a big, stone wall
with that horse? Ian tells him, "Yes, because he's all of 17,
and brawny." Dad dares him, "Just show me, I bet you can't!"
Ian takes a circle with his shiny, prancing stallion, another faster
circle, and heads straight for the stones scrambled on top.
I close my eyes. Silence, horses snorting, a moan.
Ian is off, the horse is gone, and there is blood. Dad grabs me
off Conroy and hands me his reins to hold with mine.
Looking up, all I see is black ovals of noses, froth blowing
in and out like a spiderweb in a hurricane.
Dad leaves me. I stand stock still. I always do my job.

Life

You get a chance to find a partner before the music begins.
Usually you are young and wide-hipped:
mango ripe.
Slippery in the choosing.
Looking for wariness, bicep curls and safety
as one can be fooled by the scent of lust.

It's life– then you dance:
it's a hip bending back swaying errata series
and you wonder if you are making an impression.
Like the movie star ladies with heavy breasts
on the sidewalk in Los Angeles.

My mother says, "Listen to the music."
"Sit below men and look into their eyes so they are convinced
you believe in their strength and that you have none."
I sit below them listening and I see pouches of disappointment,
eyes full of mistrust,
memories of mothers like me,
and my hips are frozen: transfixed.

The music in life is temperamental.
I am a dancer
with no partner.
My hands are marked with large, fat veins
transgressing each other.
Working so hard at refreshing me.
Sometimes, I push on one hoping it will back up,
form a pool: an untapped source of joy
I might slide into for a time.
A kind of folding chair at the side of the room.

Riding

Take me for a ride in your big German car.
Let the windows slide up over the world,
and we glide all over the city, not talking.
So silently and smoothly as I sit in the leather molding, like a Hapsburg princess
bowing and waving to my sidewalks.
Take me in your big German car to Soho
where we can eat in places with names like countries that have abbreviated
themselves into booths and red leather seats and shared dishes served by
waiters with hair that is curled into spires of cities yet unknown to me.
Turn on your woman who tells you where to go, how to navigate the
world, with a voice that is low from under the dashboard, almost guttural,
so strict you do it even when I ask you not to.
Take me in your car on the highway above and around the city lights
and we glide along you, and me, with the place between us
and the purr purr of the great German machine telling me not to
worry until morning. There's music to be heard from azure squares, and the BBC
world
makes everything all right,
the proper perspective as
I braid my hair,
polish my Alpen rose,
lower my lederhosen, while you drive us into the night.

Remembering Isadora Duncan

I asked for a womb with
a view.
Just a small picture window
to see what was coming.
Even then I wanted
to be prepared.
I think about routes before
I take them,
Conversations
before I have them
and life before I
live it.
Even the garden
Is not spared from prediction
As all I do is prune and refuse
to replant.
They think I dance for myself
But all I do is planned.

Pay No Attention to the Man Behind the Curtain

In summer it is a good thing to travel with hand luggage,
eat fruit colored orange by the sun somewhere else.
Sleep on white sheets,
avoid things needing long periods of chewing, and
arguments.
Swim underwater and open your eyes,
play ocean noise over and over,
the waves like an angry lion's paw
on the beach.
I am interested in stopping time.
Yesterday on the airplane I saw a woman repeat herself
walking up the aisle.
She was older and yet
in a younger costume thinking it would make her life begin again.
There are wild rose hips here and it isn't even Ireland. No one
touches them.
The lone dog wanders the beach.
I wish I could see my father's hand again and tell him what I think
and this time he would listen.
There is someone in the room turning the round ball
holding the bingo numbers and I am waiting for B 61.

Barnstorming

When I was 29 and carrying a daughter, I dreamt you made me
fly with you again.
This time we took the old 1923 Breezy Biplane.
I sat in back:
a perfect view of your neck lines: road maps of unattained destinations,
unsatisfied longings, angry firebreaks cut into a surface of skin.
Turning repeatedly, you yelled over your shoulder, forcing me to listen
as you flew over barns, houses with windows, happy
families that angered you and made me wistful. I
wished for a parachute, but then I always did,
hearing all the ways I had failed you as a daughter.
Up ahead there was an open barn that you spied late in the ride,
gleefully pointing it out to me.
"Watch! I can fly right through that barn and never hit the walls!"
I never doubted you and watched the wings carefully place themselves inches
from the shaggy barn sides.
In an instant it was over and we were flying straight up.
You with your gnarled teeth bared and me with my baby.

Melania

Melania reminds me of mean Barbie:
You know the one I mean....
You never play with mean Barbie
as you can't talk to her like the others.
You have no idea what her voice would
sound like so you leave her respectfully
in the box.

Lord only knows where she's from but someplace tough. You don't even remember who gave you mean Barbie. You do have a hunch. So many people can't connect with kids or anyone for that matter. Giving mean Barbie to a kid is like invisible punishments: you know they are coming but you don't know when or where. Or what you've done.

I have great sympathy for Melania. I may be the only one in California that does. I'd like to know what bargain she made to keep dressing like mean Barbie and holding the hand of the Donald. What is she thinking when she has that expression on her face that makes her look like Cruella Deville? Is it all about money? What would it have been like for her if she just had married a normal guy who couldn't afford beautiful clothes?

I'm hoping that there's a reason that's very compelling, that she's doing this other thing just to be the first lady. It's one thing to be the first lady to Barack Obama but it's quite another to be the first lady to Donald Trump.

Maybe she has a plan. Maybe she thinks there's some tiny way she can make things better in the world. I hope so. People gave me mean Barbies and I never took them out of the boxes. They made me nervous. I have a really hard time with people who are living a disingenuous life. I'm lucky because I have the advantage of being able to live a genuine life.

It's easy if you lose someone that's a part of you, and your heart breaks and nothing is ever the same again and you keep hoping that you imagined the whole thing but you know you didn't. Living a genuine life is the only way you can live after you'v suffered great loss. Things become clearer

And it's annoying to a lot of people. But the good news is you really don't care. Truth is a liberator and I guess that's the benefit of pain.

Letter Yet Unsent

I still see the back of your silvered head as you play
chauffeur and drive me away from my two
weddings in the antique car only you could drive.
You
were dead by my third wedding so my husband and I never
left the reception believing we could keep the marriage
together by staying on, not dancing. Though the last words you said to me were
"You are a loser with one misfit for a child and now you will have two more!"
I remember the smell of your houndstooth coat when my nose
snuffled against it and the way your tongue
lodged quite carefully in the left-hand corner of your mouth
when you danced with our mother, our beauty.
I remember the X-Rays of her ribs taken at the E.D.
where I took her with pneumonia and the doctors asking
how she broke them and don't worry she never said one word.
I remember your top dresser drawer with thirty different compartments,
each filled with the necessities of your life; peppermint lifesavers, shirt stays,
bullets, silver dollars, black socks, THINK books, matches from the Stork Club,
Kodachrome film, 50 white handkerchiefs and a stack of hundred-dollar bills. I
remember the shape of your calloused nail beds snarled
like angry crabs always scrabbling at the world and its people.
Looking back now, I can see your eyes and remember a time
when I wasn't afraid of you and that is what I am building on,
and each new day I will remember what you were before you were born,
before you learned to speak and not to love.
I'm writing to you now to tell you I have forgiven you, almost, and I
who have looked so hard for love am ready to gently come upon it.

Sweet Strings

Andre Segovia had the power to lighten the dark,
restless mind
in the casing of a father.
Only Andre with his strings so sweet
could unbind the cerebellum,
loosen the limbic system, and
awaken the pineal gland,
making his pale eyes water into light.

Home from work
at seven,
a limited time offer of good humor,
the record turned and we watched:
hoping the power would fail
before he asked one of us to dance.

Our mother hiding in the small intestine of the house
digesting roughage,
taking purgatives,
painting her face with war.

Oh Andre:
I am thinking,
when I hear your notes today,
what would I look like now
if we had been safe?

When I Think of My Mother I See a Closed Door

When I think of my mother
I see a closed door, and a long, gray
hallway with soft, almost colorless,
carpet and in the afternoons of dead leaves and
silence I say to her now,
"Let me in to sit by your dressing table
with potions and lotions and rouge by Revlon
with 'Cherries in the Snow' faintly printed on the back
in black cursive."
"Let me watch your beloved fingers caress your face as
if they were from a lover you once knew and lost."
"Let me know why you linger last on your lips, so carefully
arcing the stick first one side then the other over and over
while your lips wait, upturned, for you to be through."

I ask you to turn and see me, sitting here
watching, learning, practicing,
how to be alone.

Part Three

I've Found Her Lost Again

In the dusky, damp hour of summer when wine
is poured and in the distance neighbors
bicker over their barbeque, the husband saying
it's not his job to clean it and clattering
the domed lid over
five pounds of grade A beef.
The wisteria, desperately holding itself open
to possibility, and the dogs roam barking, their
tongues sloppy with grass. The birds, repeaters,
warble from tree to tree, trying to vary their story,
back and forth, back and forth, so bored with each other.
In the yard a pool filled with azure water, an aquarium of
tears, piss, semen, a pure rectangle, a holding pond of life,
there, lying on the surface, on the great,
pink, plasticized, inflatable swan floating unguarded,
there's a girl. She could be 19 or 70. She's listening to
the opera of summer, writing a bird libretto, her fingers
holding the minute hand on the clock of time, suspended
by the undercurrent of oboe, she knows she's different.
She feels every rhythm.

Filial Visit

My son picks me up in his snail-shaped car and we head south:
past the silt of San Jose and past the blue/brown mountains.
He drives like he was still in Italy and
tells me how he felt when he was 12, 13,
14, and 15.
Weaving through the highway with his elbows out and his fingers
gnarled about the wheel,
he tells me how he had no friends and how mad he was at me.
I say I am sorry, and I wonder if that is enough to say about
getting divorced.
He says he wasn't lonely just that everyone else was screwed up,
and I know eating won't be possible tonight.

Then, just before we reach Carmel, he says how strange it is to
be here,
the place where he spent four years of school,
and that he forgives me.
He knows it wasn't my entire fault now. I am afraid to breathe.
I am happier than I can remember and I smell the wood smoke
outside
and the smile of the hotel porter makes me fall in love.
I kiss the amenities in the bathroom as if they are gold,
frankincense and myrrh.

We sit at the bar, and he talks about flying jets in the Navy,
going through the stages as if he were describing a physics
experiment.
I say I want him to do a "fly by" over my house every once
in a while
so I can look up and feel my breath inspire me.
I don't think I could love anyone more in this moment.
The love feels so fragile and delicate I can't look at it
as it fills me with fear.

The Wedding Veil

In our family we have a wedding veil saved by our grandmother.
It is yellowed, has small curls of lace woven into it and a scalloped edge.
The bride wears it on her head like a hair band.
Lace scallops are stiffened on the band and circle her head like a
crown of thorns, or one of those metal halos spine surgery patients have on.

Brides in our family that have worn the veil are divorced,
yet we preserve the veil after each wedding,
have it carefully repaired by a lace expert,
boxed up by a boxing expert,
and then decide, as a family, who should store the veil.

Now, it is stored in my house.
I suffer from an overwhelming sense of responsibility.
What if there is a fire?
Would I remember the veil?
The box containing it worries me like impending hurricane clouds.
My daughter asks me if she should wear the veil
and I weigh the odds:
antiquity versus reality.

My sisters like to know the veil is safe,
yet no one wants to be veiled.
The keeper of the veil
is the keeper of the curse.

Gratitude

Today a 72 inch round table arrived in a large white truck
driven by a very young curly haired man with white teeth who
was very agreeable to unpacking the table and unwrapping the paper
and bringing it into my garage for future parties.
He admired a small red fire engine toy that I had held onto for
40 years and I gave it to him.
You would have thought I had given him a priceless diamond.
I heard him calling his wife as he walked to his truck
describing what he was bringing home to his four-year-old son.
My heart swelled in my chest so I couldn't breathe
for a moment and I thought to myself
gratitude works.

Pale

People around me are fading
paling. So quickly.
Yesterday your eyes were so light
I could see Naples in them.
Before I knew it I was sipping Chianti
on that small porch on the loggia
behind the hotel.
You were bent over your book
legs crossing the width of the terra-cotta tiles
siphoning the warmth of summer from them.
Your hands so strong and wide around the book.
I was thinking about later
when the air cooled
and your head in my lap
we would be colorful again.

Sable Night

It looked as if tonight were a sable night.
The coat had been removed from the coat closet
in the deep basement
by the husband and curled in readiness
on the foot of her chaise lounge. Ready to snarl and pounce.
Ready to slink and saunter.

There was a party at the museum:
black tie and she was getting ready.
Sitting on the edge of her sink peering into the mirror myopically,
she wondered how he decided these things and if her eyes
were wandering?
Both at once.

She waited for the jewelry arrival delivered on a tray
just like a caviar service or a scalpel,
and listened for the sound of his heels
clicking along the rarest of mahogany,
clicking into her heart with his ability to impress
even now, even now when she knew her worth,
even now when the markets were down,
even now when she hadn't been touched in months.

In the end she danced with all
the company heads, all the corporate loan officers,
most of the competitors, glistening
all the while in her curated perfection.

Vermont: Fall's End

Lying in a bath in Vermont in the early evening
with a small candle and a wet dog in the corner,
she wonders
if the man downstairs she came here with
is as safe as the warm bathwater and the rain falling to music.
The window is divided into ticktacktoe squares
misted from the heat.

In the warm bath she watches the oil and water
play with one another
breathing in lavender while she breathes out fear
adding hot water every few minutes.
She watches her body appear
through the soap and water letting her belly rise like a small mountain
and her toes peek back: as disembodied little villagers
looking for supper.

Tonight, there will be dinner and family to meet.
They will bring magnifying glasses and notepads.
The man has begun to peel back her heart
and she practices putting it back together
just to make sure she can when he leaves.

48

Murmuration

"A rare gathering of starlings that looks like dancing clouds"
passed over my head this morning like a shiver in a graveyard.

Murmuration:
the sky darkened, my dogs slowed their pace, and I still

struggled to hold up the dike against the flood of winter.
My mind pushed back the chill of late fall, back

against the solitude coming, the harsh quiet of the snow.
As long as I'm moving, I can't remember you

but in winter the mind releases its starlings
and there you are, suddenly, in all your glossy magnificence,

and here am I, alone.

In the Desert You Can't Remember Your Pain

In the December desert near the crepuscular
hour many people experience subtle, ocular
change. Sometimes these changes are
permanent. Saguaros cactus (Te
quiero) can begin to move
and appear to challenge with their arms the
delicate prickly pear while the Feather
cactus plays catch a falling Star. It is, however,
the Christmas cactus that interests me:
blooming blood red pink like a baby's lips exactly at the
time they say we had a virgin birth.
Who will tell it to do that now that we have lost faith
a world divided, no party lines, no Avon lady, no
agreement not to kill each other.

Theft

I watch you from behind a great gnarled oak tree, its
roots dug into the cement of a city. My
hands press against the bark, reading the braille of
betrayal. I'm hiding and watching like a falcon floating
for rats and I don't want to watch but I have to.

Here you come out of the backlit brass arch of a door of 825 Fifth Avenue
your arm circling around her, your faces turn in unison towards the new awe
between you.
I watch. I cannot stop watching.
I watch the tilt of her head and the angle of your missing heart.
I watch the swoop of your suited arm confusing her with its warmth,
a promise of safety like a magician or Jack the Ripper.
I'm watching. I cannot stop watching.
Six hours ago, I was that woman
under your spell.
Six hours ago, we had tomorrow.

Conclusions are Lethal

Conclusions are lethal so I keep searching, not wanting to close the book
on the marriage, I'm collecting evidence like Nancy Drew or Sherlock Holmes
and, Damn! I'm good. Unearthing scraps in the caller ID, empty drawers
(former home of boxer shorts, unused bullets, scraps of paper, loincloths).

I'm not ready to stop yet. My sister asks how I feel when I do this. I tell her
bad and I cry. I know there will be a conclusion someday and it will come like
a rock thrown through my window, and there I will see the glass shimmering
around me all on the floor like diamonds, each piece a time I cried for him:
his hands, his eyes, his body. Frightened the conclusion
might be he never loved me is why I keep digging. These secrets will be all
on the table laid out like dinner so they can't jump and bite me like a scorpion
hidden under the bed or maybe a woman named Victoria he lied to me about.
I'm going to wail "Why" a few more months: "Why" into the night. "Why" in
my car and "Why" when I find his old jacket in a closet and I carefully
remove it, gently lay it on the floor of my kitchen and lie on top of it.
He's still there. I can feel him.

Naptime

In the soft, smooth part
of the August afternoon
in the summer house on the upper floor someone listens
to the quick inhale of arousal across the hall.

Sticky smooth heat
melting bodies into one another:
breast into breastbone, belly against belly, thigh laying onto thigh,
thick and sheen-ready scent of earth soil,
deep bergamot, violets and rain all
twist across the hall into the single room unfolding into a banner
of loss.

The guest from New York lies
on top of a single bed,
hands folded and open book
folded over breasts.

There is an ache beginning in her heart
she will ignore, so used is she
to ignoring this ache.

The banner of love scent will taunt her:
wafting around her left nostril until she is forced
to turn onto her left side
place her nose into the deep starch of the pillow.

Even then there is a glimmer of memory,
a glimmer of the present,
a glimmer of the moment when she forgot she was alive.

If I Hadn't Asked

If I hadn't asked who you were having dinner with that night, I
wouldn't be crazy lost now and you wouldn't have moved to
Connecticut with an eyebrowed cooking woman: something I
would never be.

If I hadn't asked if you liked sleeping alone maybe
we would have grown accustomed to each other sighing
into our dreams, a hip teaspooned into a hip, yours so much
fuller than mine, sailing on into the night, no navigational devices needed.
Bacon for breakfast.

If I hadn't read her emails maybe I could have forgotten the alert messages
coming almost daily into my cerebral cortex. Messages telling me the ice was
thin though it was late summer.

If I hadn't asked why you were leaving maybe I would still believe you
did love me, though now I see all I need to do is be silent and I'll
never learn that.

1963, Connecticut, President Kennedy, Cuba and My Dad

Before the house sold, I go down into it, down
the rubber-treaded stairs still squeaking at me,

down into the basement watching my feet change
from the pointy-toed splendor of 2015 into red Keds, dirty-

laced, and I'm an Iroquois again treading softly, listening to
the distant drumming of war songs.

The old bomb shelter remains and it's still 1963
and the Cuban Missile Crisis holds our family frozen.

Everyone has a job to do so we can survive.
Rows of bunk beds like saltines overlapping

in a cellophane rectangle, neat stacks of claustrophobia, sealed
containers of food: beans, rice, dried soup, water, peas,

petrified they will be brought to life again.
I open some up and am relieved to see everything

is still intact, in place, ready to sustain. Parcheesi next to Band-Aids,
Monopoly still monotonous. We never played games as

real life required too much attention, but my parents were hopeful.
I see the air powered by continuous peddling on the stationary bike.

I sit on it once again and pedal. I am immediately tired.
I remember the drills, the duck and cover, the lie of it to us kids who knew

we could not be saved by a desk as radiation would find us like a
greedy hand reaching under the doors and into throats and the handgun

hung by the door, loaded for the neighbors who would want in.
My father's plan to save us written out in longhand on doors, pasted on

cabinets, read and remember, duck and cover, stay alive for me,
it's not safe out there. I still hear his words and want to tell him
it is safe now but it's too late.

North Haven Island

A family floats every summer,
on the Island of the warm and hopeful.
Electricity runs to each homestead:
filling bedrooms with current events.
The bay around contains the fragile with circling currents
while trodden paths define the limits
of their lives.

There is a house for every child:
some old, some new, some mortgaged,
some with memories not in safes,
some with memories denied,
replaced by wishbone walls.
Construction so brittle every word is heard,
every wish, forsaken.
At daybreak gulls cry the auk of sorrow.
At night ravens savage the lavender of sleep.

There are boats in the harbor
with navigational devices guaranteed to find the mainland,
they always fail.
Some families float for centuries,
bobbing on Penobscot Bay directed
by whales and dolphins
eating sea crusts
speaking no evil,
the language of darkness.

There is an annual summer tea
where all return to drink chocolate
and defer whipped cream
and hold their hands to their eyebrows
searching the horizon for amazement,
and when it arrives
refuse to feel it.

Grief

I'd write about alcohol, but instead I'll write about trees,
as when felled, they tell all their truth. Buzz saw
a tree and there is her soul laid out in concentric circles:
years of aimless joy, sunlit afternoons of umbrella splendor,
minutes of wild leaf dances and seconds of shivery wetness there
before your very eyes, and you cannot resist touching the
inside of her splendor.
There, too, is the evidence of straw-sipping dry spells, desperate
root tips, and so many years of thirst gone unnoticed.
The long lonely winters which froze certain limbs,
lost forever to the forest foragers.
A tree tells the truth in the end.

Love at the Car Wash

I met a man at the car wash.
Before I knew it, we were having sex
in the waiting area
and I thought to myself that his beard,
which had seemed so impossibly prickly
was, in fact, soft against my lips, chin, belly and
when we lay together behind the corrugated
shed of rinsing, streaming, water, he said he would
follow me anywhere even though he was nearly
70. I thought to myself, my life all along had been building
towards this moment of pure desire for me for him:
for water for breath for earth for stone for trust.
Later, I tipped Bob and climbed into my car
and noticed how clean it was and how the rear-view
mirror showed me a man I could love and I thought
"What a day for a daydream!"
And I drove home.

The Dinner

She arranged her breasts as offerings to the night:
lifting and presenting them in lacy cups
and set out to stir the sauce.
Salty and thick, some wine for headiness, she added oregano
and took out the no.
She was going hunting.

The prey was so beautiful: curved and elegant, haunches still young,
and eyes, eyes so filled with information
about things she never knew she wanted to know.
She sat with him and the other guests and lowered the table so the eyes of
the guests were on each other
and no one knew what was happening in the other
world, the underworld.

His leg was so stretched out to her that her ankle became a radar
communicator,
a depth sounder.
Above board there were still rules
but in the underworld of love
there were none.
It was hot.

The dinner grew and the outside doors opened and vines and sweet fog
came in from the garden,
and one man asked his dinner companion to open her mouth.
There was a type of music playing.
The table was lifting and desert was so sweet no one could remember
anything but the taste of it in their mouths.
No one wanted to remember anything.

Interviewing

I met two guys who know how to fix stuff:
make things out of wood,
rescue women and children first,
keep a fire going,
laugh at farting and cry at war.
But they were taken.

I am interviewing men.
I have been continuing this process since January of 1995.
There have been many applicants.
Some more entertaining than others.
You have to watch carefully to determine
if they have a cage or a box or
maybe, a behavioral book
on their person.
And, oh yes, look at their tongues
for forkedness.

I have thong underwear,
a lie detector machine,
an American Express Platinum card,
invisible children,
an enormous library,
a Sonic Care toothbrush,
a fast car,
caller I. D.
and an endless capacity to giggle.

I am tired.
Just as I say I am giving up,
up pops another offering.
I am a sucker for nice hands.

In the end I say
here are some poems to read
and they walk away into the night,
white sheaf of paper, a broken wing under their arms.

Creation

She wants to hold his head in her lap and, each hand holding a side, pull it split-open, precisely so each cerebellum would be encapsulated like a walnut inside a split shell. Then she would hold up first the left side, and then the right, so close to her eyes she could see what was black and what was right. Then she would look into the tiny pineal gland of the future and take the pulse of his darkness and test the depth of his wounds.

She wants to take his head off his body and replace it with one that looks just like him and carry it home to put on the kitchen counter right between the flour and the sugar. She wants to further examine him using the ear thing and the light and peer into his feelings and his history of loyalty to pets and his willingness to brush her hair until they both crackle.

Then she wants to choose which side she likes best and she wants to go to her linen closet where, behind the pillowcases, she has other split brains.
She chooses the left side of practical abilities and from the right she chooses lust but they don't go together correctly.
So, she goes to a psychiatrist and asks him to
put them all back together because now it is a big mess.
She forgets what she really wants.
She confesses she longs for the way it was in the beginning.
Then she was back where she started.

Seeing Lake Tahoe

Seeing Lake Tahoe for the first time made the cones and spheres
inside my eyes spin and leap in excitement
stimulated by the electric blue,
and the sharp, bright harshness
of the sun within the lake.

Afterward, things were never the same.
I remember thinking maybe my eyes had to be brought
to life like Sleeping Beauty with the Prince's kiss.

That weekend I began to see things that had been
background noise before and there was no turning back.
My husband's hand on another woman's ass,
My daughter's limp hair falling to silver collarbones
sitting like a necklace someone loaned her,
the neighbor's cigarettes smoked out on the back porch
always alone, accompanied by a glass of Gin.

In the morning the long, hot, dock calling me
suspended above the eye-changing lake,
lifeguarding what was left.
Everyone wanted to be blind.

I Love My Gun: A Confessional

I love my 28-gauge Beretta over and under shotgun.
It came in a green case with leather
straps strapping it in.
The case makes one think of medical instruments
or maybe shoes for very tall thin people.
When you open the case there is a compartment
for everything.
This is one of the reasons I like it.
Small square places for chokes
and long narrow places for barrels,
my gun has two barrels that are interchangeable:
one for small kills and the other, for big.

I like to open the case and look at
all the compartments filled up.
Sometimes I lift up a barrel and smell it:
oil, powder, dirt, explosions.
I often do this before breakfast.
I wonder why I am not ashamed.
I shoot flying clay discs
into shards for an archeologist to piece.
I am comfortable shooting.
I hold the gun like a "born shooter,"
says James,
an ex-marine wife-abuser deer-killer who teaches me.

We walk along paths
wearing camouflage gear,
brown human clothes with hats and boots
and one can hardly tell we are not human.

James has huge leather pouches of
ammo strapped to his trim waist
like a male Scarlet O'Hara.
When I shoot he never says "Good" but
"Kill" when the disc shatters over primeval preserves.

There must be a genetic flaw here.
You don't have to tell me.
As soon as I got the gun I felt powerful:
long and cool

ready to engorge.
I could stroke it in its case
and put it away in the closet.

Bird's Eye View of Flight

In the middle of his life
he became a bird,
hooked by a whooping crane.
One morning in the slow fog of northern Florida,
swept south to the keys,
swinging over marshes like a circus act,
distended by humility and wind,
he was carried by the large crane who ate
only on rainy mornings, mashing down fish still alive.
He was home-schooled in observation,
exhalation, and weather prediction in crowds.
Being suspended in flight
is actually comforting, he found.
He floated, held under his arms by the feet of the kind crane,
hooking around him like handcuffs with padding.
The crane only wanted company and to stretch out his legs.
The man had no control of anything.

Thanksgiving

Suddenly:
a flock of small, black birds
swoops over the pond,
like a magician's cloak, snapping.
He blinks.
She sees the birds as a sign:
refusing to blink, she watches the flight.
She has missed her flock now
and will have to remain here.
They are both standing on the wall
above the pond wearing sweaters
with wreaths knit around their necks.
A hawk dips with a long hook,
dips down just over where they stand.
Then, he is gone, towed up and away.
She doesn't remember blinking.
In one moment everything changes.
She is alone.
He is thin air.
Her sweater begins to unravel
on its own.
People say they are sorry.
She can't tell them how he left.
No one will believe a hawk could tow away
a man.
But in this case, he was weightless
and forgettable.

The Neighbor

Each morning the dogs walk her down Chestnut Street.
Past Taylor's house, empty lot, red mower for sale ($95.00),
Mrs. Alonzo's dead flower bed, and she's got makeup on and
clothes that are good because it's time to wear the good clothes.
There's Bob with the two white poodles prancing and Bob prancing
because he can when he's out of the house.
She always stops at the empty lot, stares at the two abandoned rattan
chairs and wants to slip into one, take a breath from dancing all night,
sip the last of her champagne.
She still hears music.

Getting Around Town

It was late morning when she first forgot
where she lived, and deep November in northern
Vermont, and the car heater was still working,
puffing prodigiously on the way to town.
Crossing her eyes with desperation in the post office,
she turned away from the simple white paper with cold black lines
and drew a rabbit on the Formica table
lying like a mortician's tableau
below her.

She turned her head very slowly as an owl does
(not disturbing the hump in her spine),
when wondering who you might be,
her owl eyes clicking
a slow semi-circle to the left of the line
of mailers,
waiting to post money or love,
hate or anger,
give or take,
she was looking for who she was.
She would be any of them
in the blink of an eye, if they would let her.

Slice of Life

A boy and a girl walk downhill this
morning as I'm walking up,
all perfumed and waxed,
shaved and shaped by early morning
tumbles into each other roughly,
still not understanding pleasure.
Not touching but each intently staring
at small devices as they walk, she in her
silk flowered, flouncing playsuit and he with his baseball
cap pushed back on his buck toothed face flushed.
She looks up at me gently when I say out loud
"Look up! You are missing the world!" and
laughs like she's been caught eating the good
chocolate and he keeps walking and texting,
walking and texting.

Diagnosis

The moment
the doctor turns to you and says, rather sorrowfully,
"There's a small problem,"
the moment when your body doesn't belong to you.
You nod, appearing to listen carefully,
there is a churning inside you louder than any small part
of Niagara Falls and you can't hear what she is saying.
Maybe if you make her words into Scrabble letters, hard and square,
you could jump on her quickly while the door is still closed
and force them back inside her mouth,
hold her nose and sit on her chest,
rumpling her white coat
until she opens her mouth and agrees to swallow.
Make her the one with the small problem.

She appears not to notice when you begin to cry.
You have to ask for Kleenex.
What you would really like is for her to be older and more sympathetic.
You would like her to offer you tea
which she would have ready behind her desk
on an old lace doily her grandmother made.
She pours the tea, takes your hand, and tells you no matter what
she will take care of you. That you will survive.
There will be no fear in her voice when she says this.
Nor will she look at her watch.
You will sip the tea together
and you will gather your things and leave.
When you go to sleep you will dream of one stone on one beach in Maine.

The Great Blue Heron

He flew in under the cover of darkness,
folding his wings in an envelope of marsh and beach grass,
waiting to allow me
the pleasure of his return
until morning.

In the dampness of November
the heron's message of surprise
is a secret gift I tell no one about.
The heron knows me like no other
and he returns just when the night seems too long.

As I sip my coffee in my slippers on the lawn
the heron watches:
deciding when he will show his great deep beak
and his broad blue wings above me,
deciding when he will fish for me
or reveal a sliver of sun on this gloomy day
in the beginning of winter.

The heron knows he belongs south but he is a loyal bird.
Refusing to take to the air on time,
he is my guardian: my winged seraph,
the keeper of my pond there in the early morning
with the steam of the earth raising her young.
The heron is the first one who knows I need him.

Almost 70

Tomorrow I met a man.
I recognized his hips
and the lean of him. I wanted
all of it.
I can't keep secrets.
They slip out of me
when I'm not looking
falling onto magnolia leaves
and people hear them
so I'm keeping this lust
to myself until I find it.

What I Really Wanted for Breakfast

The damp, warmly tropical smell
of the wisteria vine planted Thursday,
that I passed early today,
scent like a Venus flytrap
capturing my practicality
tossing it out of my mind.
Then images of dim, early morning bodies:
Damp and tangled sheets,
inner hip skin and the
taste of salt.
Otherwise, I'd have been fine
but for that vine.

Under It All

Under the coral sweater
designed by Gianni Versace
sits my elegant heart beating.

I have two lovers: difficult
to choose from as some weighty, ripe pomegranates.

Sing me a prayer with your hands on my
breasts, take me where the other hasn't.

Make me rejoice in my choice
but not forget the sound of his oboe.

Combine the two into a garden that welcomes
Puck and weeds,

let me hear the music of weeping
and not look back.

Adoption

I remember when I was young and beautiful but at the time
I thought I was fat and boring. Maybe my mirrors were bad or
my astigmatism was uncorrected.
Now I think I am bewildered about what I did in my life
and why I stayed where I stayed.
I have written to the British royal family and asked them to consider
adopting me. I think I would be a good addition as
I know how to dress and have beautiful table manners
and I really feel comfortable with a strict schedule.

I would know instinctively how to back out of a room, and how to
occupy myself during the daytime hours.
I would certainly never embarrass anyone and I like the idea of
knowing what was going to happen for the next 7000 days.
I love dogs so I would fit right in.
I look good in riding clothes even though I am 70 but the horse
always knows I am afraid of him.

I don't think it's a lot to ask of the royal family because
they need help and so do I. It's a very equitable solution for all.
I don't need a title though I would like a crown. I like the idea
of living in a house with many other people who have no idea
how many people are actually living In the house. It's the idea
of all those bodies there that brings comfort
and the prescribed nature of life which is soothing.

CPSIA information can be obtained
at www.ICGtesting.com
Printed in the USA
BVHW021039041020
590255BV00015B/113